MONDAY
MOTIVATION

MONDAY
MOTIVATION

*52 Lessons for Living
the Best Year of Your Life*

A Little Book with a Lot of Power

Second Edition

Kathleen DuBois

Published by Progressity, Inc.
One Bridge Place
10 Hale Street
Charleston, WV 25301
www.progressity.com

Second Edition
ISBN 978-0-9838237-1-1

This book is dedicated to Suzanna and Madeline Teel.
Thank you for bringing sunshine into my life.

Introduction

Dear Readers:

Personal growth is a rewarding, life-long journey that almost always involves some level of discomfort. What I know for sure is that having the right attitude makes all the difference. Running away from difficult situations holds back our growth. Tackling adversity head-on can make us stronger and more dynamic than ever.

Over the years, I have coached numerous individuals and teams on how to improve their results and achieve goals. What I've learned is that in order to help others be their best, I've got to do the necessary work on myself to be *my* best. Yes, it's true!

My experiences have revealed that most people don't know how to create a better life for themselves. If this sounds familiar to you, then this book will surely be of assistance. The purpose of *Monday Motivation* is to provide food for thought and practical exercises for people who want to be more fulfilled, live a higher quality of life, and become better versions of themselves.

Thank you for sharing in the belief that we all have the power to design the lives of our dreams.

Here's wishing you happiness, love and prosperity.

Kathleen

How to Use This Book

This book is an easy-to-use guide that reveals many secrets to manifesting positive results in your life. You can study the lessons and do the exercises over and over again for years to come.

The best way to tap into the benefits of *Monday Motivation* is to focus on one lesson per week. However, if you want to ramp up your success, feel free to study two or three teachings each week. Ideally you will brew up a cup of coffee or tea each Monday morning and set your intention to implement the assigned *Call to Action* throughout your entire week.

You can work through the lessons sequentially, beginning with Lesson 1, or randomly select lessons from the book at your discretion.

To help you gain the maximum benefit from this *little book with a lot of power,* I've created a free, downloadable workbook that you can print and put into a three-ring binder. Go to www.KathleenDuBois.com/MondayMotivation and click on the "Download PDF" icon.

As you move through the weekly teachings, write out your *Call to Action* exercises and jot down any thoughts that arise. Writing initiates thinking, and thinking moves us into action. Therefore, the process of writing out the exercises is an essential element to generating positive movement in your world.

You will notice some overlap and repetition in the exercises. This is purposeful. Repetition is the key to learning and opens your doors to personal growth.

Finally, one of the most effective ways for you to receive value from this book, in addition to reflecting on the lessons and doing the activities, is to share what you are learning with family, friends, and colleagues. I want to particularly encourage you to pass this material to children. These lessons are powerful for people of all ages and the earlier a person integrates them into their life, the better.

Enjoy the journey.

Acknowledgements

Throughout my life, I have been surrounded by amazing people who have believed in me, often when I didn't quite believe in myself.

I would like to acknowledge six incredible mentors and teachers who have significantly influenced my life in positive ways: Samuel Bonasso, John Hanna, David Hardesty, Jr., Paul Hutsey, J.R. Keener and Edward Robinson. I hope to inspire others as much as these gentlemen have inspired me.

I also want to extend a sincere thank you to my compadres at Progressity, Inc. (www.Progressity.com). My brother-in-law, Michael Teel, has served as our creative director since 2001. He designed the book cover and gave me incredible encouragement to make this project a reality. Michael is the type of person everyone needs on their team, and I can hardly put into words the value he has brought to my life, both personally and professionally. Thank you to Melissa Maki and Kaitlyn Hill for editing my manuscript. Their expertise and kind feedback are so appreciated. And thank you to our designer, Chris Spence, for all of your support with both my book and KathleenDuBois.com website.

Finally, I want to acknowledge all of my faithful *Monday Motivation* readers who have taken action in their own lives and shared their amazing stories of transformation with me. You are the inspiration that keeps me going every day.

Part One
Self-Awareness

"

..."

Have the courage to say no. Have the courage to face the truth. Do the right thing because it is right. These are the magic keys to living your life with integrity.

–W. Clement Stone, Businessman, Philanthropist, and Self-help Author

Lesson 1
Do the Right Thing

Courage, truthfulness, and integrity are qualities shared by the people I admire most.

One of my mentors once told me that the hardest word in the English language to speak is "no." Saying no, nada, zip requires bravery. Authenticity requires that we set ourselves apart from the masses.

A number of years ago, I worked with a colleague who would never stand up for herself and say no to others because she was afraid of rocking the boat—even when rocking the boat was the right thing to do. Consequently, she lived life in conflict and inner turmoil. Her actions were not aligned with her beliefs.

Doing the right thing and not following the crowd can be tremendously difficult, but the payoff is infinitely rewarding. In fact, when we examine truly successful people throughout history, what guided them toward their victories was having the courage to say no to the masses and staying focused on doing the right thing for themselves and others.

Think about it.

Call to Action

Are you in a situation where you are struggling to do what you know is right? Do you find yourself in a position where you feel certain that saying "no" is absolutely the correct way to go? Step out with conviction this week and do the right thing; say the right thing. Others will rise up to encourage and support you. And you'll strengthen your integrity, that's for sure.

"
●●●

*Honesty and transparency
make you vulnerable.
Be honest and
transparent anyway.*

– Mother Teresa, Catholic Nun and
Nobel Peace Prize Recipient

Lesson 2
Honesty and Transparency

Being honest and transparent can feel downright scary because it means revealing one's true nature. It so common place for people to mask their vulnerability and pretend to have the world by its tail.

Every time I go out on a limb and share challenges I'm experiencing with trusted people in my life, they seem compelled to be honest and open with me about their own difficulties. When we have the courage to let people know that our lives are not perfect, we discover a level of emotional freedom and authenticity that helps us attract positive opportunities.

I'm not saying we should air our pain and dirty laundry every day in forums like Facebook, but I am saying that hiding behind a facade is no way to live. Life is too short to not live it with openness and honesty.

Think about it.

Call to Action

Are you hiding something about your life you should share with a trusted friend, colleague, family member or professional advisor?

This week, reflect on an aspect of your personal or professional world where you can be more transparent and authentic. Write down your thoughts and commit to having an honest communication with someone, whether written or verbal. This revelation may cause you to feel vulnerable, but the rewards will be worth the effort.

" "

• • •

Knowing others is intelligence; knowing yourself is true wisdom.

**—Lao-Tzu in Tao Te Ching,
Classic Chinese Text**

Lesson 3
Self-Awareness Is Powerful

People often analyze others—family members, friends, and coworkers—pinpointing their attributes, particularly their weaknesses. Judgments are made about other's behaviors and beliefs. Images are concocted about who other persons truly are. Yet the same people spend little time analyzing themselves.

About five years ago, I set out on a course to truly study myself. I hashed through why I did the things I did, and the motivation behind the decisions I made (good and bad) over the course of my life. I got real clear on my weaknesses, strengths and true desires. Whoa! What a mind-blowing process!

Inner discovery leads to self-love, which is absolutely essential for a rewarding life. Of course, getting to know oneself can be a difficult and challenging process. What a better world it would be if we spent more time looking inward to examine and enhance ourselves and less time judging other people.

Think about it.

Call to Action

This week, write down five to ten words or phrases that accurately describe who you are at your core. Make note of both your positive attributes as well as the traits you don't like and hide from others. If you feel compelled to do so, share your list with a trusted friend or family member and ask that person to provide input as to the accuracy of what you wrote. Reflect on your list daily in an effort to get to know and ultimately embrace yourself. Each day, look at yourself in the mirror and say, "I love and accept all parts of myself."

> When we feel love and
> kindness toward others, it
> not only makes others feel
> loved and cared for, but
> it helps us also to develop
> inner happiness and peace.

–The Dalai Lama, Buddhist Leader

Lesson 4
Love and Kindness, Happiness and Peace

My staff and I have established a weekly tradition in our firm. To start our week off right, every Monday at 10:00 a.m. sharp, we gather around the conference table and share one thing for which we are grateful. It can be anything ranging from: "I'm grateful for the wonderful weekend my family and I had," to "I'm grateful for the big contract we just won." Typically our expressions involve kind words in support of one another. It's amazing the positive and productive energy this transmits throughout our work environment because of this simple, yet powerful, weekly sharing process.

Displaying intentional acts of love and kindness to our family members, friends, neighbors and coworkers is such an easy thing to do. And it's much more rewarding than spending our energy criticizing others. A simple shift in our thoughts and actions can make all the difference.

Think about it.

Call to Action

Spread sunshine into the lives of others this week by practicing a random act of love and kindness each day. To keep you on track, make a list of five things you intend to do this week that will express love, kindness, and appreciation to others. It could be as simple as bringing your coworker a fresh cup of coffee and a smile. You'll soon find that small acts of kindness can reap big rewards.

"

...

Change the way you look at things, and the things you look at begin to change.

–Wayne Dyer, Author and Self-help Advocate

Lesson 5
Perspective

A friend recently said to me, "I cannot wait until this year is over. It's been terrible." In my usual optimistic fashion, I immediately encouraged her to tell me ten great things that had occurred in her life this past year. She went on to begrudgingly share that she received a raise at her job, her daughter had a baby, and she got herself out of a bad relationship. Voilà! Once my friend changed her perspective and realized that some really incredible things had occurred in her life, the year in review didn't seem so awful.

When we experience a difficult season in life, it's common to focus on what went wrong rather than what went right. Simply shifting how you look at things can change your entire outlook and fill you with positive feelings. Scientific research has proven when we feel better, we make better choices. While I don't necessary believe that everything happens for a reason. I do believe we can find a lesson in everything that happens to us.

Think about it.

Call to Action

Devote some time this week to writing down everything that has gone right for you in the past six months. Completely refrain from noting anything that went wrong and only write down the positive. Reflect on your list this week (and any week moving forward). Express gratitude. You will feel so much better.

" "

• • •

Being miserable is a habit.
Being happy is a habit.
The choice is yours.

–Tom Hopkins, Sales Trainer

Lesson 6
The Habits of Misery and Happiness

One of my favorite childhood storybooks is *Winnie the Pooh*. As a little girl, I was continually intrigued by Eeyore, that loveable little donkey who goes about life in a perpetual state of gloom and doom.

Many of us have an Eeyore or two in our lives. I bet their names just popped into your head right now. On the upside, many of us also know individuals who are habitually upbeat and brighten a room like walking rays of sunshine. I think it goes without saying that living in a state of happiness is much more productive than living in a state of misery. Although each emotion has its place, you should aim to spend more time in a position of joy rather than misery.

Habitual sadness and happiness are choices in attitude that we make every day. Each of us has the power to live a good life. It's all in the choices we make.

Think about it.

Call to Action

Research indicates it takes twenty-one days to break a habit. If you are in the routine of being miserable or negative, make the decision today to shift to a more positive perspective.

This week, be mindful of your negative thoughts, words, and actions. This exercise takes a lot of mental muscle, but I'm going to ask you to write down any negativity in your thoughts and actions. Then enlist a trusted colleague or family member who you spend a lot of time with to point out when you appear unjustly negative. Doing both of these exercises will help you to consciously recognize the negativity that stems from your inner self and help you to move past it.

"

...

*We must let go of the life
we had planned, so as
to accept the one that is
waiting for us.*

–Joseph Campbell, Writer and Lecturer

Lesson 7
Letting Go

When I was a high school senior, it was common to write in our yearbooks about how we envisioned our lives unfolding in the future. I wrote with conviction that I would own a flower shop and have seven kids.

I do own a business, but it's certainly not a flower shop, and the only child I have is of the furry persuasion, a Westie dog named Charlie. Although different than what I had planned at age eighteen, my life is still amazing. Along my journey I've had to let go of the early vision I had for myself—flower shop, seven kids, and all—to accept the incredible life that was waiting for me and continues to unfold.

How about you? Look back on your last ten years. Did you think you'd be somewhere or someone different than you are today? Perhaps you are saying to yourself, *I thought I'd make more money by now, or I thought I'd be retired by now, or I thought I'd be happier by now.* If so, it's time to make a mental shift. Welcome the life that is waiting for you with open arms. Let go and accept. It's very powerful.

Think about it.

Call to Action

Take time this week to reflect on something in your life which didn't turn out the way you hoped it would, something you really need to release. Are you clinging to the fact you don't live where you thought you'd live? Or brooding over a relationship which didn't work out? Or maybe you are harboring anger toward a colleague or family member whose choices negatively influenced yours? Whatever the case, do yourself a favor and let go. Just let go, accept, and open yourself to the wonderful life that is waiting for you. It's possible!

> The secret of health for both mind and body is not to mourn for the past, not to worry about the future, or not to anticipate troubles, but to live in the present moment wisely and earnestly.

–Buddha, Spiritual Teacher and Founder of Buddhism

Lesson 8
Living in the Present

Do you ever stew over what went wrong in the past or mourn the loss of people, things, or opportunities? Do you fret about what might or might not occur in the future?

Guess what? The only moment you truly need to focus on is *now*. The past is gone; it's history; it's over. Tomorrow, next week, and next year have yet to come, and worrying about what may or may not occur is not a good use of your creative energy. Allow your past to serve as a teacher, and let thoughts of your future serve as inspiration. Living mindfully in the current moment is one of the greatest gifts you can give to yourself and others. Then sit back and enjoy the present.

Think about it.

Call to Action

If you are holding on to pain from the past or worrying about the future, I have a great activity for you. Take a pen and paper and write down your worries and heartaches. Then have a "letting go" ceremony. Toss that piece of paper in your fireplace, fire pit, or even your barbecue grill and watch as your worries and heartaches burn up in flames and disappear with the smoke. The freedom of letting go and focusing on the now is a wonderful feeling. Trust me, this is a very liberating exercise!

"

"

• • •

It takes twenty years
to build a reputation and
five minutes to ruin it. If you
think about that, you'll do
things differently.

–Warren Buffett, Businessman and One of the
World's Most Successful Investors

Lesson 9
Your Reputation

The decisions and actions we make every day, all day long, affect our reputations. Living a life of honesty, integrity, and kindness strengthens our reputations. In contrast, lying, making poor decisions, and treating people badly can negatively affect how others perceive us. How many times have we seen the reputation of a public figure go up in flames due to one awful decision or action?

We have all read one story after another of a famous sports, political and entertainment figures whose fans were crushed when the truth came about about some really bad behavior. The reputation sting is so bad that sponsors drop them like a hot potato. Then it takes months and years, even a lifetime, to rebuild the solid reputations they once had with the public.

While everyone makes mistakes in life, we build a solid reputation by living a life of honesty, integrity, and kindness. In addition, how we respond to our mistakes truly matters. Life gives us many opportunities to build character. Open up to the lessons, and you will flourish.

Think about it.

Call to Action

Conduct a reputation checkup this week. Take some time to ask a trusted colleague, friend, or family member about how they perceive you in the areas of honesty, integrity, kindness, and authenticity. Write down their comments and determine if there are any changes you want to make in your life. This activity takes courage, but it's a wonderful opportunity for self-reflection and growth.

" "

• • •

Carpe diem.

–Latin Phrase

Lesson 10
Savor Today

Carpe diem is Latin for "seize the day." I love this phrase. In fact, just saying it out loud inspires me. So many times we allow our days to pass by without any joy, passion or meaning.

Isn't it interesting how we pine for yesterday and long for tomorrow, yet we rarely savor today and all of the opportunities it holds?

Since we never truly know what tomorrow will bring, having a daily mindset of seizing the magic today has to offer can truly shift the way we feel and act. And when we feel good, we're more likely to attract good people and opportunities.

Making time to intentionally be in the present can make all the difference in our lives.

Think about it.

Call to Action

Try this activity to increase your awareness of the power of living in the now. Take out a piece of paper and write down issues from the past you hold on to. Next, write down issues which may occur in the future that cause you to fret. Then rip up the piece of paper and commit to living in the present this week, one day at a time. Carpe diem!

"

...

*Be who you are
and say what you feel
because those who mind
don't matter and those who
matter don't mind.*

–Dr. Seuss, American Author and Cartoonist

Lesson 11
Who Are You?

For years, I've been teaching a graduate-level marketing class for West Virginia University. One of the standard assignments I give to students is an exercise that requires them to define their own brand, their unique identity. I am always surprised at how personally insightful this activity is to each student.

Who we are is so much more than our family roles and what we do for a living. Oh, the blank stares I receive when I simply ask the question, "If you take away your job and your role in your family, who are you?"

It's interesting how most people go through life without really knowing who they are, what they stand for, the passions that inspire them, and how they want to be remembered. We identify ourselves by our jobs, our family expectations, how much money we make, and the type of cars we drive. But in fact, we are none of these. Our goal should be to live an authentic life and that our real identity be expressed from our very heart and soul.

Taking time to describe the elements of your true self is so powerful. When you operate from a point of authenticity, a sense of peace and joy will surely follow.

Think about it.

Call to Action

Give yourself a gift this week, and take time to write down your answers to the following:

1. What five words or phrases describe your authentic personality?

2. How do you want to be remembered by others?

3. What makes you stand out among others?

4. Describe your unique physical characteristics.

5. On what topics do you consider yourself a subject matter expert?

6. What do you excel at and love to do (e.g., leading others, gardening, public speaking, being a mom, or fixing cars)?

Though this exercise may feel awkward at first, working through it and reflecting on the results can be the beginning of understanding who you are and who you want to become.

" "
• • •

If you are unhappy with the results in any area of your life, the person responsible is always available for consultation. And guess where you'll find them? In the mirror!

–Paul Martinelli, Motivational Teacher

Lesson 12
Happy or Miserable? You're Responsible!

We often blame others or external factors for the level of happiness or unhappiness we experience. Believe it or not, we are totally responsible for our own joy. This concept is difficult to accept, because it is much easier not to take responsibility.

I'd like to offer three powerful life lessons that apply to both personal and professional situations:

1. We can't change other people; we can only change ourselves.

2. Blaming others gets us nowhere.

3. We are fully responsible for our own attitudes, choices, and actions.

We have the power to live the lives of our dreams by simply embracing self-responsibility. When we blame other people and situations for our misery, sadness, distress, or any other negative emotions, we give away our power. In contrast, taking total responsibility for the quality of our lives creates an indescribable sense of peace and contentment.

Think about it.

Call to Action

Ask yourself if there's something negative occurring in your life. Write down whatever you come up with. Then take a look in the mirror and ask how you, and only you, can make the situation better. Write down and reflect on your solutions, and get ready for positive changes to occur in your life.

If you find yourself backsliding, keep close to the mirror, take a long look at yourself, and repeat these words, "I am responsible for any unhappiness that I experience in my life, and I have all the power to shift my perspective."

Part Two

Goal Setting, Habits, and Gratitude

" ... "

Surround yourself with only people who are going to lift you higher.

–Oprah Winfrey, American Television Host, Actress, Producer, and Philanthropist

Lesson 13
People Who Lift You

When I was growing up, my parents always encouraged me to hang out with positive friends. There's a reason why: the people with whom we surround ourselves have a definite influence on both our attitudes and our results in life.

Business philosopher and motivational speaker Jim Rohn once said that we are an average of the five people with whom we spend the most time. How about you? Are you surrounding yourself with the right people? Do they inspire you to unleash your inner talents and become a better version of yourself? Or do you spend your time with people who drain your energy or display negative attitudes?

For the most part, you choose the people who surround you. Why not select great people whose very presence and energy makes you want to be a better person?

Think about it.

Call to Action

Make a list of the people who have a significant presence in your day-to-day world. This includes family members, business colleagues, and those who are often present in your thoughts. Determine whether these individuals lift you up or drag you down. If it's the latter, it's time to make a change. I strongly suggest you strive to spend at least 75 percent of your time with people who lift you up. You'll eventually see the benefits and find yourself reaching higher and higher.

" "

• • •

Never let discouraging
people and discouraging
situations talk you out of
your dream.

–Joel Osteen, Author and Pastor

Lesson 14
Hold Tight to Your Dream

The ability to envision dreams and bring them to fruition is a remarkable gift that each of us possesses.

Do you have a big goal or a heart's desire that you are pursuing? Maybe you want to start your own business, to land a promotion, to meet Mr. or Mrs. Wonderful, to get healthy, to write a book—the list goes on. Whatever dream you hold on to and work hard for, don't let others discourage you. Don't let setbacks get you down. Know that you possess the ability to achieve greatness.

Years ago I had a dream to start my own consulting firm. A person who I greatly admired told me I was crazy. He wasn't a dreamer and didn't understand me at all. At the time, I didn't know one thing about launching a business. However, I held tight to my vision, surrounded myself with amazing mentors, took many leaps of faith, and got my company off the ground on October 5, 2001. Now I work with an incredible team, serve inspiring clients, and smile with joy every day as I walk into our office. I'm here to tell you that dreams can come true when we refuse to allow discouraging people to bring us down.

Think about it.

Call to Action

What's your dream? Take some time to write it down. Be very specific. It is essential that you devote time to your dream every day. Surround yourself with people who can help you achieve your vision. Secure any specialized knowledge or skill required. Success always requires action. Happy dream hunting. It can be an exciting ride!

" "

. . .

Everyone has an invisible
sign hanging from their
neck saying, "Make me
feel important."
Never forget this when
dealing with people.

–Mary Kay Ash, Businesswoman and
Founder of Mary Kay Cosmetics

Lesson 15
Make Others Important

When I feel important to my family, friends, co-workers, and clients, I'm on top of the world.

Psychologists and human potential experts all agree that the true sense of self-importance comes from within. However, acknowledgement from others is a need that all humans possess.

What I know for sure is that each of us has the power to uplift others by saying or doing things that help them feel special and important. When we focus on spreading positive feelings to people in our lives, we magically begin to feel better ourselves.

A client of mine hosts motivational seminars in women's prisons. She reports that her attention to these inmates makes them feel empowered and valued. Throughout her two-day seminars, my client witnesses many of these female inmates transforming in the way they see themselves, because they are being acknowledged as important.

Even simple acts of recognition and words of affirmation can help people feel better about themselves.

Think about it.

Call to Action

You can make a big difference in someone's life this week. Write down the names of five to ten people, or more, who really matter to you. Then either pick up the phone or find an opportunity to look them in the eye and say, "I want you to know how important you are to me." This simple act of kindness will go a long way for both of you; trust me on this one!

"

...

*To be a champ, you have
to believe in yourself when
nobody else will.*

–Sugar Ray Robinson, Professional Boxer

Lesson 16
Believe in Yourself

It's incredibly powerful to believe in yourself. If you have a burning desire to achieve a personal or professional goal, stay the course and don't let anyone derail your excitement.

While success never occurs in a vacuum, and connections with others are essential to achieving your goals, the most important ingredient is that you believe in you. Keep any self doubt in check when it starts to creep in.

Orville and Wilbur Wright are two of history's best-known dreamers. They had a burning desire: to make a machine that would allow them to fly through the air like a bird. Many people thought the two brothers were crazy. Orville and Wilbur crashed and failed over and over again, but they never lost faith in their vision and abilities. The result was an invention that revolutionized travel. Can you imagine what our world would be like if the Wright brothers had given up on their dream?

Think about it.

Call to Action

This activity might seem a bit awkward at first, but it's powerful. Write down *I believe in myself because:* at the top of a piece of paper. Then list ten reasons why you believe in *you*. Totally disregard what other people think. You'll be a big believer in you in no time!

" "

• • •

It is our choices that show
what we truly are, far more
than our abilities.

–J.K. Rowling, Author of the *Harry Potter* Books

Lesson 17
The Power of Your Choices

From the time we rise in the morning to when our head hits the pillow, we make tons of choices every day that influence our results in life.

While J. K. Rowling has become astoundingly famous for her *Harry Potter* books, what really intrigues me is her rags-to-riches personal life story. In five short years, she progressed from living on welfare and being plagued with depression, to celebrating multimillionaire status and living the life of her dreams. While in turmoil, Rowling had an idea for a book, and she eventually made the choice to act upon it. That single choice to *act* made all the difference.

Successful people make the right choices and persist, particularly when they experience unforeseen blunders or roadblocks. It's those right choices, even more than our abilities, that determine our results in life.

Think about it.

Call to Action

What choices do you need to make this week in order to manifest improvements in your professional or personal world? Is there an issue you need to step up and take responsibility for? Do you need to let go of a bad habit? The choices are endless. Choose one issue to focus your energy on this week and write it down. The great news is that you own your choices; no one can make them for you.

66 99

• • •

A smile is an inexpensive way to improve your looks.

–Andy Rooney, Radio and Television Writer

Lesson 18
The Magic of a Smile

The power of a smile is amazing. I grew up in a family of picture takers. In my household, we constantly yelled the words, "Say cheese!" as Dad snapped the camera.

Motivational consultant Debra Moorhead said, "The most overlooked and undervalued human asset is the smile. Movie stars spend thousands of dollars on their smiles because they know a great set of pearly whites will pay off in the long run. Do any of us realize the true, raw power a smile gives you?"

Smiling has great significance, both in our personal and professional lives. Flashing a grin helps overcome barriers and open doors for people. A sincere smile is a message of positivity and is considered a sign of goodwill and confidence when dealing with friends and colleagues. Not to mention that when you feel downright miserable, there's nothing like a smile to immediately shift you to a better place.

Think about it.

Call to Action

This week, notice how often you smile. In addition, be mindful of whether you surround yourself with people who smile. As you take all of this in, keep flashing your pearly whites to as many people as possible. You'll soon begin to understand how positive and infectious this simple expression can be. Happy smiling.

" "
. . .

If you don't know where you're going, any road will get you there.

–The Cheshire Cat from *Alice in Wonderland*

Lesson 19
What Are Your Goals?

It's impossible for us to achieve great goals in life if we don't know what we want. How can we complete a road race without a firm finish line? And what would happen to the game of football without an end zone?

I've found most people don't really know what they want out of life. They are unfulfilled, coasting along with the status quo. It is essential to define our desires in life and create a road map to achieve them.

A great goal has six elements. It is specific, measurable, and achievable. It also stretches us out of our comfort zones, stimulates excitement within us, and has a deadline. Each of us possesses amazing power to set and achieve goals.

You, and only you, can chart the road map for your life, so why not make it a fulfilling and exciting one?

Think about it.

Call to Action

This exercise is ongoing and will most likely take more than one week. Brainstorm achievements you would like to realize in your life. You might set a goal to get a college degree or to publish an article. When you feel ready, write down three to five personal goals. As you jot down your thoughts, make sure that each goal has the six elements listed above. To make progress, it is essential to establish an action plan and deadline for each goal. Since this is such an intense exercise, I provide additional information in a downloadable workbook on **www.KathleenDuBois.com/MondayMotivation**.

Happy goal setting.

" "

...

The antidote for fifty enemies is one friend.

–Aristotle, Ancient Greek Philosopher

Lesson 20
The Magic of Friendship

I am a very wealthy person. I'm not referring to the balance in my bank account; I'm referring to the balance in my *friend* account. Friendships, both professional and personal, are vital to a happy life, and they are priceless. True friends support us during tough times and celebrate with us through the good times. We should never, ever underestimate the magic that a friend brings into our lives. Their presence is powerful.

One of the darkest times of my life was when both of my parents passed away within four months of each other. A team of amazing friends drew me out of the shadows. I had friends who checked in on me constantly, who offered to help run my business so I could take a break, who listened to me pine away for my losses, and who sat with me during times when I felt just plain sad.

What I've come to learn is that in order to *have* a great friend, you must first *be* a great friend. Take this simple lesson to heart. When you focus your intentions on being a wonderful pal to others, you will receive endless benefits that flow to you as easy as a hot knife through butter.

Think about it.

Call to Action

Write down a list of your closest friends, and reflect on what each one brings to your life. Write about why you consider each of these persons your friend. Become mindful of the many areas of support they provide and ways they enhance your life.

Next, get ready to increase the balance in your friend account! Let each person, whose name you wrote down, know how much you value your relationship. Spread the love.

" "

• • •

Gratitude is riches.
Complaint is poverty.

–Doris Day, American Actress and Singer

Lesson 21
Are You Rich or Poor?

How do you achieve true happiness? The answer is simple. Be grateful for what you already have, right here, and right now.

I work with clients every day to help them identify the good in their lives and in their organizations. When this mind-shift occurs, more opportunities seem to appear.

Yes, life is sprinkled with pain and difficulty, but when you recognize positive aspects of your being, whether it's family, friends, or material belongings, you might find yourself suddenly saying that life is good.

A mindset of gratitude is like a magnet to happiness and contentment. What I know for sure is that almost everyone has an abundance of reasons to be grateful in life.

Think about it.

Call to Action

I firmly believe in the power of a gratitude journal. Do yourself a huge favor this week; buy a notebook or journal and title it *My Gratitude Journal*. For one full month, write down at least five things each day for which you are grateful. If you're having a bad day and can't think of anything to write down, try something simple such as: *I'm thankful I can breathe* or *I'm thankful I can get out of bed each morning*. Remember, there's always something in your life for which to be thankful.

" "

. . .

I've always been in the right
place and time. Of course, I
steered myself there.

–Bob Hope, American Comedian and Actor

Lesson 22
Right Place, Right People

Success requires being in the right environment, with the right people, at the right time.

I'm always in awe when I look at a mighty oak tree and reflect upon the fact that it grew from just a tiny acorn. If you place an acorn in fertile soil with the right amount of consistent light and temperature, it can grow to more than one hundred feet. On the contrary, you could place that same acorn in the cold ground of Antarctica, and it wouldn't sprout a fraction of an inch.

How about you? Are you placing yourself in a healthy environment, with supportive and inspiring people, so that you can flourish? Are you consciously aware of the places where you choose to spend your time and the people with whom you surround yourself? Open your eyes to this lesson, because most people don't realize the powerful shifts that can occur in their lives by steering themselves to the right places, occupied by the right people.

Think about it.

Call to Action

Draw a vertical line down the center of a piece of paper. On the top left column, write the headline *The Right Environment*. On the top right column, write *The Right People*. In the left column, list all of the places where you flourish. As an example, my list includes: my office, church, my home, and out in nature. And for me, *The Right People* includes: my family, best friends, and colleagues at my firm.

Once you have completed your list, position yourself in the right places and with the right people more often, and reduce the time you spend in the wrong places with the wrong people.

"
...
"

The only place where
success comes before work
is in the dictionary.

–Vince Lombardi, Legendary Football Coach

Lesson 23
The Ingredients of Success

Why do we think success is supposed to come easily? Truly triumphant people spend a great deal of time sharpening their knowledge and skills, putting in sweat equity, and building positive habits. They do so to the degree that most people think their success came easy, but that's rarely the case. When we do things we love, such as pursuing an inspiring goal, the hard work doesn't seem so awful. My firm just started its twelfth year of business. For the first seven years, I must have worked eighty hours a week to build a strong foundation. Today things are always changing at our firm, and I am still putting in a lot of time and effort, but success comes much easier now.

How about you? Are you willing to do the work to get where you want to go? If so, get ready for amazing results to manifest in your world.

Think about it.

Call to Action

Pretend you have fast-forwarded your life twenty years.

Then, imagine you are looking back on the previous twenty years and write about the successes as if you have achieved them. One by one, write out a concrete action plan to carry out in order to manifest a life with those successes.

Live your life knowing that success takes effort, and then all of a sudden, things will become easier for you.

"

...

"

*If you can dream it,
you can do it. Always
remember that this whole
thing was started with a
dream and a mouse.*

–Walt Disney, American Film Producer,
Voice Actor, Animator, and Entrepreneur

Lesson 24
Dreams Do Come True

I meet many people who feel uncomfortable with dreaming and goal setting; it's almost a foreign idea to them. In reality we have all been born with the ability to imagine—that includes you, too.

All great things in life start with a thought, mental picture or an idea. Of course, the manifestation of a dream requires persistent action, but it all starts with the big and little ideas we create in our minds.

When was the last time you clearly envisioned your dream job, your dream house, your dream physique, your dream relationship? If Walt Disney can make a dream come true, so can you!

Think about it.

Call to Action

Let your mind fly and complete the following sentence.

My wildest dream is to...

Be very specific. Write down that wild dream and pay attention to how you feel during the process. An example might be: *My wildest dream is to travel to all seven continents with my family in the next five years,* or *My wildest dream is to get in excellent shape and win a strong woman (or strong man) contest.* If you're willing to dream and to take persistent action, you can make your wildest visions come true. I've seen it happen over and over again!

> I dream my painting,
> and then I paint my dream.

–Vincent van Gogh, Dutch Post-Impressionist Painter

Lesson 25
The Power of Vision

All great accomplishments and works of art start in the mind. It's inspiring to hear Van Gogh's words on the power of visualization.

There is a common trait that all highly successful people possess: the ability to picture something crystal-clear that does not yet exist in reality. President John Kennedy visualized a man walking on the moon. People thought he was out of his mind. Trips to outer space are so common now that we hardly pay attention to them.

I recently built a new home. My ability to visualize big and small details, along with having an incredible contractor, helped me to create an amazing haven for myself. The colors, furniture, and art in my house are a total reflection of who I am. Most importantly, during the construction process I envisioned my home being a great gathering space for family and friends. Today, I experience so much joy hosting dinner parties, happy hours and holiday gatherings with those I love. What dreams will you paint on the canvas of your life? You have the ability to be your own Van Gogh.

Think about it.

Call to Action

To make your dreams a reality, take the first step and clearly describe them in writing. What kind of job do you want to have? What type of house do you want to live in? How much money do you want to make? What type of difference do you want to make in this world? The questions go on and on. Once you have your dreams laid out, take each day this week to reflect on your dream list and begin to visualize with carefree creativity. Ask yourself what actions you can take to begin achieving your dreams. Know that one small step toward success can begin to change your current reality.

> " "
> ...

Nothing can stop the
man with the right mental
attitude from achieving
his goal; nothing on earth
can help the man with the
wrong mental attitude.

–Thomas Jefferson, Third U.S. President and the
Principal Author of the Declaration of Independence

Lesson 26
Unstoppable Attitude

Does your mental attitude *help you or hold you back* from achieving your goals? If it's holding you back, realize that you, and only you, have the power to select your attitude and the actions that follow.

My niece, Suzanna, had an unstoppable attitude about getting a puppy. She carefully researched various breeds for months. She talked to her parents again, and again, and again, about how she would be a responsible dog owner. Suzanna saved her money, and then researched and talked to her parents some more. She zeroed in on a specific breed called a Lhasa Apso and was unstoppable in her pursuit of a puppy. One day, Suzanna and her family went to the pet store just to look and guess what? They came walking out that afternoon with a furry ball of energy and named her Chloe. Today, Chloe brings everyone in Suzanna's family so much laughter and joy. You have total power to possess the right mental attitude. Don't put it off another day.

Think about it.

Call to Action

Attitude is a combination of our thoughts, feelings, and actions. Join me this week in doing an attitude checkup. Is your attitude in harmony with the person you really want to be? If not, you might want to think about readjusting it. Since there are so many things in life we can't control, it's great to know that we have total control over our own attitudes.

66 99

• • • •

Confidence is going after
Moby Dick in a rowboat
and taking the tartar
sauce with you.

–Zig Ziglar, American Author, Salesperson,
and Motivational Speaker

Lesson 27
Confidence

Feeling confident means you are certain of your skills and ability to succeed. It is an internal determination or judgment of how sure you are of yourself. The good news is that belief in oneself can be cultivated throughout life.

A healthy dose of confidence is a key ingredient to success in both your personal and professional worlds. I'm not talking about arrogance; I'm referring to a solid belief in yourself.

When you feel a strong level of self assurance, you become willing to take action despite opposition. You are more willing to take risks and go the extra mile, admit mistakes, and learn from them. A healthy dose of self confidence allows you to get back up when knocked down, and know that success will eventually come in some shape or form.

Think about it.

Call to Action

Do yourself a favor this week, and take time to complete this activity.

Make a list of ten things that give you confidence, ten things you do that make you feel *great*. For me, exercising regularly, taking a risk on something or someone, and delivering a winning presentation give me confidence. Everyone's list is unique. Recognize what actions give you confidence and do those things regularly.

" "

...

Behind every communication problem is a sweaty ten-minute conversation that you don't want to have.

–Gay Hendricks, Psychologist and Writer

Lesson 28
Tough Conversations, Positive Benefits

The "sweaty ten-minute conversation" refers to the difficult communication you know you need to have with an individual or group but can't initiate due to fear of what might occur.

Mustering up the courage to have that uncomfortable conversation with a boss, co-worker, family member, service provider, or friend can change your world for the better.

My friend Anna shared her experience of having a difficult conversation with an employee who continually missed deadlines and delivered subpar work. Anna agonized for days and finally had the sweaty conversation. The result? An apologetic employee who agreed she'd been slacking on the job due to personal turmoil. The employee felt empowered because of her own courage to communicate with truth and honesty, and in the end both Anna and her employee strengthened their relationship.

The moment you have that tough conversation, you gain the instant reward of relief. More importantly, you open up a flow of communication which will allow you to address instances of conflict or inner turmoil.

Think about it.

Call to Action

Define a sweaty ten-minute conversation that you've been putting off. Make a commitment to initiate that communication this week. In preparation, take fifteen minutes to write the issue down and make certain you're clear about what you want to communicate with the other person or group.

When you decide to have the talk, tell the truth, tell it quickly, and tell it with kindness. Oh, and remember to put on an extra layer of antiperspirant that day!

" "

...

The number one reason
most people don't get what
they want is that they
don't know what they
want. Clarity is power.

–T. Harv Eker, Motivational Speaker and Author

Lesson 29
Clarity

We are conditioned from a young age to believe that dreaming and shooting for the stars isn't necessarily a good thing.

Consider these questions: What kind of a house do you want to live in? How much money do you want to make? What's your dream job? What type of professional and personal relationships do you want to have? How do you want to be remembered when it's your time to leave this planet? My list of questions could go on and on. The point of this lesson is unless you know what you want, how in the world are you ever going to get what you want?

Most people let life happen to them. You have the power to create the life you desire, and the first step starts with you generating a crystal-clear vision of what you want. All opportunities and experiences are created twice, first in the mind and then in reality.

Think about it.

Call to Action

Grab a piece of paper and write down the following seven categories, leaving space to write underneath each one:

1. My Relationships

2. My Home

3. My Job

4. My Income

5. My Lifestyle

6. My Service to Others

7. My Health

Under each category, let your imagination fly. Define what you really want in each particular area. Remember, you have the power to create the life of your dreams—it all starts with knowing what you want.

" "

. . .

Every child is an artist.
The problem is how to
remain an artist once he
grows up.

–Pablo Picasso, One of the Greatest Artists
of the Twentieth Century

Lesson 30
Your Inner Artist

Oh, the power of creativity. It stimulates new ideas, an inner feeling of excitement, and a mindset that anything is possible. Recently I spent the afternoon with my two nieces who are nine and twelve years old. We were eating ice cream at our favorite local parlor, and out of the blue, one of the girls said, "What if everything in our world was made out of food?"

Suzanna and Maddie imagined buildings made out of cheese, trees of broccoli, and cars manufactured from bananas with doughnut wheels. The ideas went on and on. We laughed as we dug deep for ideas on how roads, sidewalks, and even street signs could be created from edible items.

This creative conversation made me think. Why does out-of-the-box thinking get stifled? When was the last time you imagined with the unrestrained passion of a child? As adults, we can get bogged down in life by practical limitations and responsibilities. We forget to let our minds go, to have fun, to consider endless possibilities.

How different things might be if dreamers were taken more seriously and held in higher regard. What I know for sure is the people who dare to think differently and imagine wild ideas are the people who truly make a difference in our world.

Think about it.

Call to Action

Take some time this week to stimulate your creative thinking. Are you ready for a fun conversation? Get together with your staff, a best friend, or your family and have a creative brainstorming session just for the fun of it. For example, if you had the chance to make your own movie, what story would you want to tell? Would it be a comedy, drama, or thriller? What type of characters would you create? Who would you pick for your starring roles? Write it all down, and relish in the experience.

" "

• • •

Whether you think you can or can't, you're right.

-Henry Ford, American Industrialist,
Founder of the Ford Motor Company

Lesson 31
Can or Cannot?

One of my all-time favorite books is *Think and Grow Rich* by Napoleon Hill. The book was published in the 1930s and is the culmination of Hill researching five hundred of the world's most successful people. While these 500 individuals disagreed on many specifics as to what makes a person successful, they all agreed on one thing: we become what we think about. This idea has been written about for centuries in works such as *Pygmalion, The Little Engine that Could, As a Man Thinketh,* and the list goes on.

About two years ago, I started documenting negative thoughts that popped into my head when I would get frustrated about accomplishing something. Then I would immediately write down an opposite, more positive thought. What I discovered by consistently doing this exercise was my whole world shifted for the better. If this can work for me, it can work for you, too.

What you think about repeatedly becomes your reality. This philosophy works for both positive and negative thoughts. So when you start getting discouraged about accomplishing a goal or overcoming a hurdle, emulate The Little Engine that Could, and make a decision to choose the thought: "I think I can, I think I can, I think I can…"

Think about it.

Call To Action

For one entire day this week, keep a notebook with you from the time you get up in the morning to the time your head hits the pillow. Jot down any negative thoughts that pop into your mind. For example, "I can't stand my job," "I can't pay my bills," or "I can't seem to lose weight." Then write down a more positive, opposing thought using the word "can" instead. "I can find a more fulfilling job," "I can figure out how to pay my bills," and "I can change my lifestyle and lose weight." When you complete this exercise, I can almost guarantee that you'll start to feel better. Believe in YOU.

"   "

. . .

*If your actions inspire others to
dream more, learn more,
do more, and become more,
you are a leader.*

–John Quincy Adams,
Sixth U.S. President

Lesson 32
Everyone Is a Leader

Leaders come in all shapes and sizes. As a young girl, the leaders who influenced me the most were my parents, teachers, Girl Scout troop leaders, and cheerleading coaches. Every day, we each have the opportunity to exercise leadership abilities and inspire others to be better versions of themselves.

As John Quincy Adams says in this week's quote, anyone who helps others dream more, learn more, and do more is a leader. Children, teens, and adults alike are influenced by leaders and are leaders themselves.

Great leaders are curious, possess the ability to think independently, and have a strong desire to inspire others. They surround themselves with the right people, set personal and professional goals, and seek out mentors and coaches. They look for opportunities to take others to a higher level.

You can help make this year your best one yet by stepping up your leadership abilities: become a more inspirational parent, manager, volunteer, friend, spouse—you name it.

Think about it.

Call to Action

This week, I encourage you to conduct a leadership checkup. Think about your role as a leader by reviewing the following questions. Then write down your answers to these questions:

1. Who am I responsible for leading (e.g., family, employees, church group)?

2. How do I take those I lead to a higher level?

3. How am I continually working to be my best?

4. Am I trustworthy to those I lead? Why?

Then, celebrate your strengths as a leader and fine tune any areas for improvement.

Part Three

Dealing with Adversity

When I thought I couldn't go on, I forced myself to keep going. My success is based on persistence, not luck.

- Estée Lauder, Entrepreneur and Cofounder of Estée Lauder Companies

Lesson 33
The Power of Persistence

A common characteristic of highly successful people is persistence, particularly during adversity. It is unfortunate most people give up on the pursuit of their goals when faced with trials and frustrations. Have you ever set out to achieve a goal, such as losing weight or pursuing a new job and said "forget it" when you found yourself not making the progress for which you had hoped?

Famous American country musician Garth Brooks has demonstrated the mastery of persistence. He became one of the biggest country music stars in the 90s, and yet, he didn't even win one local singing competition in his home state of Oklahoma. He tells the story of his first train-wreck of a trip to Nashville and being rejected by the very same record label that signed him years later, producing his numerous number one hits. Had Garth thrown in the towel, where would he be today? Where might country music be today?

If you have a burning desire to achieve a goal, surround yourself with people who will cheer you on when the going gets tough. Perhaps your dream is to write a book, launch an entrepreneurial project at work, achieve a job promotion, buy a new house, enjoy better relationships, or some other dream. Persistence will be the key to your success. Remember that *you* make the choice to never give up on your goals.

Think about it.

Call to Action

Write down the number one goal you are currently pursuing. If you don't have a goal, create one today. Jot down any barriers to success you are experiencing as you try to achieve your goal. Once you define these barriers, visualize yourself breaking through them. Then make a commitment to yourself you will persist and not give up.

"

...

Our finest moments
are most likely to occur
when we are feeling deeply
uncomfortable, unhappy,
or unfulfilled.
For it is only in such
moments that we are likely
to step out of our ruts and
start searching for different
ways or truer answers.

–M. Scott Peck, American Psychiatrist and Author

Lesson 34
Discomfort Leads to Comfort

It is a normal, human response to feel dissatisfied from time to time. Sometimes the heat gets turned up in our lives, and we are beyond dissatisfied, we're just plain unhappy. Such malcontent can be difficult, but it can signify an opportunity to learn and grow.

Dissatisfaction can be a healthy feeling, since it drives you to pursue a better life for yourself. Had Thomas Edison been satisfied with candlelight, he would never have invented the light bulb. Just about every invention which gives us modern-day comfort is a result of someone's healthy dissatisfaction with the status quo. It is a great motivator to get us to a better place.

When you feel stuck in a rut or are wallowing in self-pity (trust me, I've been there, and it's not pretty), remember your discomfort leads you to comfort. See every challenge in your life as a learning lesson that will take you to a more rewarding place.

Think about it.

Call to Action

Are you feeling unhappy or unfulfilled in an aspect of your personal or professional life? If so, write your thoughts down. What is the source of your dissatisfaction? What can you do about it? Writing initiates thinking. Creative thinking helps you envision solutions. It's critical to define the problem and come up with solutions so that you can move forward in a productive manner.

Grab your pen, pencil, or keyboard and get going.

66 99

• • •

Smile despite the
circumstances and laugh
throughout the pain.
Life is full of hardships
but it is how you deal with
them that will, in the end,
define you.

– Author Unknown

Lesson 35
Pain Will Always Subside

When we are in the throes of emotional or physical pain, it can seem as if the hurt will never cease. The rhythm of life, however, assures us things will always, *always* get better. The sun rises, and the sun sets; the tide goes out, and the tide comes in; difficulties come, and they slowly fade away.

During times of pain and challenge, surround yourself with caring people. Filling our minds with positive thoughts, when all we want to do is complain, makes all the difference. It takes a lot of effort to sail through a period of hurt, but the pain and difficulty are temporary and better days will surely come.

Think about it.

Call to Action

If you are experiencing any sort of physical or emotional pain right now, write down the details about how you feel because of the situation. Then identify people and resources that can support you through this challenging time. Keep writing! Finally, reach out to these people. Tap into your resources and seek support.

Know that the tides will eventually shift, and you will make it through. Something better is on its way into your life.

"   "

• • •

*When you get to the
end of your rope, tie a knot
and hang on.*

–Franklin D. Roosevelt,
Thirty-Second U.S. President

Lesson 36
Hang in There

My mother was one of the most calm, cool, and collected people I have ever known. She raised seven children with what seemed like ease and grace. Mom rarely became unglued. However, on occasion, she would let us kids know she was at the end of her rope. And who could blame her? She had seven little people running around 24/7!

Throughout the journey of life, we will come upon times when we've had it. We may even yell out loud, "I've had it!" When you don't think you can endure your difficulties, pain, or frustration any longer—hang in there. These are the times when you can learn the gift of patience.

When tough times hit, and they will indeed hit, you will do well to accept the lessons taught in the moments of frustration. Muster up all of the hope and faith you can and kick in an unwavering mindset that you can persist through the difficult times. Hang on, hang on; don't let go.

Think about it.

Call to Action

If there is any area in your life where you feel you have reached the end of your rope, write down your frustrations. Perhaps you've had it with being a parent or with your job or with your current financial situation. Whatever the case, acknowledge those extreme frustrations by writing them down. Then brainstorm different ways to cope with your challenges. Perhaps holding on to your rope requires a night out with friends, a meeting with a counselor, a walk in the woods, or a day on the golf course. Hold on tight and don't let go. Things will get better.

"

...

For every minute you are angry, you lose sixty seconds of happiness.

–Ralph Waldo Emerson, American Lecturer, Essayist, and Poet

Lesson 37
The Downside of Anger

Every day, all around the world, people are angry. They harbor anger for their spouses, their children or parents, their coworkers, their bosses, their work environments, their governments, and so many other things.

Let's turn the first paragraph completely around and start over: Every day, all around the world, people are *happy*. They are *happy* with their spouses, their children or parents, their coworkers, their bosses, their work environments, their governments, and other areas of their lives.

Doesn't the latter paragraph make you feel better?

Although anger can be a productive emotion in the appropriate context, don't let it consume your thoughts, feelings, and actions. Anger can swell and skyrocket, but you can also channel it into productive action that ultimately achieves better results.

Think about it.

Call to Action

Scan your anger vs. happiness meter this week. Write down any people or situations that make you angry.

When considering what causes you to feel angry, try to re-frame your thinking. For example, rather than being angry at your boss for something they did or didn't do, ask yourself what might they be experiencing to cause their actions. Maybe they are going through a rough patch in life, or perhaps they are completely unaware of how they are affecting you.

Then ask yourself, "How is this anger benefiting me or hurting me?" Follow up this self-inquiry by taking a deep breath, counting to ten, and letting go of your anger. Just let it go. I bet you'll feel lighter and happier.

66   99

• • •

No matter how bad it is or how bad it gets, I am going to make it.

–Les Brown, Motivational Speaker and Coach

Lesson 38
You Can Make It

Whether we like it or not, the journey of life is laced with challenges which show up unexpectedly, such as: career, relationships, money, and health. There have been times in my own life when tough situations occurred and reoccurred, and all I wanted to do was go into hiding, rather than face the reality.

Can you relate?

What I know for sure is every difficulty in life provides us with an opportunity to grow and discover what we're really made of. If you believe that things will get better, I can almost assure you things will indeed get better. This isn't pie-in-the-sky or rose-colored-glasses thinking. It's the way the world works. Faith and persistence are amazing tools to have in the toolkit of life, and they help us hold tight to the belief that you are going to make it through, no matter what.

Think about it.

Call to Action

If you are experiencing a challenge in *any* aspect of your life, write out Les Brown's affirmation on a piece of paper; stick it on your bathroom mirror and on your desk at work. Read Les's phrase to yourself repeatedly. You *can* make it through.

" "
...

*If you're going through hell,
keep going.*

–Winston Churchill, British Politician and Statesman

Lesson 39
Don't Stop!

It's true that we all experience times in our lives when it seems as if we are living in a hell on earth. At these times, we might want to hide or become paralyzed with our frustration and misery. But tough times are a part of life—sorry!

Here's the deal: life gets tough, and then it gets easy; life gets challenging, and then it's a breeze—it's a lifelong pendulum swing. Once we learn this rhythm, it's easier to get into the groove of the ebb and flow. When we accept that nothing in our world remains constant, then it's easier to maneuver through the tough times.

Just like Sir Winston said, if you're going through a difficult time, don't stop. Keep on going until you reach the other side. Going through hell makes heaven look all the more beautiful.

Think about it.

Call to Action

Write down any current downswing you are experiencing right now, whether big or small. Now envision what the upswing looks like, and write that down. Hold on tightly to that positive thought this week, and see what happens.

"

"

• • •

A smooth sea never made a skilled sailor.

–African Proverb

Lesson 40
Tough Times Make Us Stronger

Oh, life! It can be fraught with rough waters from time to time. However, just as the skilled sailor masters his or her craft by repeatedly navigating through wild storms and raging seas, we can only become champions of life by learning how to glide through difficult times. When things get choppy in your professional or personal life, view yourself as a person who is learning to become an accomplished sailor of your own ship called My Life. Navigate your future with calm confidence and be grateful for the difficulties you face. Just remember, turbulent seas always settle down, and then you can give a deep sigh of relief and assess your newfound skills and knowledge.

Think about it.

Call to Action

If you are experiencing a rough patch right now, please know that staying the course and not giving up will make you a skilled sailor in navigating the waters of life. Write down anything causing you difficulty. For each thing you write down, define something you are learning from the challenge and how you are becoming a better version of yourself because of it. See what happens!

66 99

• • •

Every adversity, every failure, every heartache carries with it the seed of an equal or greater benefit.

–Napoleon Hill, Author

Lesson 41
The Benefits of Adversity

Years ago I read a book called, *The Road Less Traveled* by M. Scott Peck. The first three words in the book are, "Life is difficult." Gee, was Dr. Peck ever right.

Life is full of peaks and valleys and while it feels much better to ride high on a wave, it's the valleys of life which offer us the greatest opportunity to transform into better versions of ourselves. Loss of a job, personal disappointment, financial challenges- these experiences are difficult but do present wonderful lessons to help us grow. It's not what happens to us; it's how we respond to situations in life which builds our character.

Doesn't it always seem as if struggle precedes triumph? For example, a beautiful piece of pottery requires firing; a precious diamond is a result of intense pressure for millions of years; and a little baby is born after hours, sometimes days, of labor pains. My point is if we view tough times as a sign of something great that's about to come, we can shift our thinking into a productive—rather than unproductive—mode. It's tough, trust me, I know, but how we view our life experiences sets the stage for personal growth and improved results.

Think about it.

Call to Action

Take some time this week to reflect upon, and write about, a difficulty you are experiencing in your life. Perhaps it's a situation with work, your health, or a personal relationship. Then write down the answer to this question, "How can I use this experience to strengthen myself or become a better person?" If you use this perspective each time you encounter difficulty in the future, you'll eventually realize that every cloud in life does indeed have a silver lining.

Part Four

There's More to Life

> If we did the things we
> are capable of, we would
> astound ourselves.

-Thomas Edison, American Inventor,
Scientist, and Businessman

Lesson 42
The Inner Genius

A powerful dose of genius lives within all of us, and that means you, too.

Studies show only three percent of the American population sets goals consistently, and these people are among the wealthiest in the country. This means most people coast through life rather than chart their own courses. Setting goals and working to achieve them provides a myriad of benefits, such as unleashing inner potential, expanding horizons, and boosting self-confidence.

According to psychologist Dr. Denis Waitley, "Dreams and goals are previews of coming attractions in your life. You are the scriptwriter, the star performer, and the producer of either an Oscar-winning epic or a grade-B movie that someone else wrote and directed for you."

The process of setting goals and taking action steps to move you in the direction of achieving your goals truly helps to unleash your inner genius.

Think about it.

Call to Action

Stop what you're doing right now and say to yourself, "I've got genius within me." I challenge you to say it out loud and with passion, even if there are people around you. Once you've belted out this statement, ask yourself, "What am I going to do about it?" Write down your answer and revisit it each day this week.

" " ...

When you're finished changing, you're finished.

–Benjamin Franklin, Founding Father of the United States

Lesson 43
Never Stop Changing

Change touches every aspect of our lives. In fact, everything in nature changes, so it's not unique to the human race.

Have you ever noticed some people create change—who flock to the very idea of it? Then there are people who run from change as if their hair is on fire.

Whether it's reorganization at work, a new baby, the end of a relationship, or a new job, change can be difficult—even if it's ultimately for the best. Unlike everyone else, champions in life fully embrace both positive and negative changes and chart a course to move through the shifts of life. Remember that you, and only you, are responsible for how you respond to the changes in your world. You choose whether to ignore what's going on or to respond to change in a productive way.

Think about it.

Call to Action

Write down one major change occurring in your personal or professional world at the moment. Then jot down your response to the shift, whether positive or negative. Finally, write a few things you know you can do to best move through the change. Brainstorm how you can harness powerful shifts in your results due to the changes taking place in your life.

"

..."

Strength is built through one's failures, not their successes.

–Coco Chanel, French Fashion Designer and Entrepreneur

Lesson 44
Failure Builds Success

The story of legendary fashion icon, Coco Chanel, both fascinates and inspires me. As a young French girl, she was abandoned to live on the streets and eventually landed in an orphanage, where she honed her skills as a seamstress. Her passion for sewing and her entrepreneurial abilities led Coco to open a small hat and dress shop in Paris. Her life story is quite a journey, and I can't help but wonder what today's global fashion industry would look like had Coco Chanel let her many barriers and failures hold her back.

How about you? Are you willing to put yourself out there to pursue a goal? Do you have the courage to fail along the way? Strength in character and ability is built through our failures rather than our successes. If you are doing everything in your power to *not* fail along the journey of life, think again. It's not about failing; it's about how you respond to your failures that truly matters.

Think about it.

Call to Action

Here's an enlightening activity. Take thirty minutes this week and write down *all* of the events, decisions, relationships, and other issues in your life that you consider failures. Write them down *by hand* on paper and feel free to laugh, cry, or scream along the way. Then, one by one, define how each failure made you a stronger person, and flex those muscles of inner strength proudly.

> *We are prone to judge success by the index of our salaries or the size of our automobiles, rather than by the quality of our service relationship to humanity.*

–Dr. Martin Luther King Jr.,
American Civil Rights Activist

Lesson 45
True Success

Isn't it interesting most people view success in life by what they *have* rather than what they *give?* This past summer, my friend Sonia and I took a day off work to volunteer at a homeless shelter for women and their families. After spending hours cooking and serving dinner for sixty-some residents, we were dog-tired physically but energized spiritually. It was humbling to serve those without a home and to realize my troubles in life aren't so bad.

To me, a truly rich and successful person influences others to be their best, lends a helping hand to those in need, gives more than he or she takes, and works to make this planet a better place.

There is so much power in giving and reaching out. If you have the blues, feel stressed, or have lost your focus, I have the cure for you: volunteer to help those less fortunate than you. You could help Habitat for Humanity build a house, spend time at your local animal shelter, or serve up a meal at a soup kitchen. Whatever the case, imagine how our world would shift if we all spent more time focused on helping others rather than building our personal bank accounts and collecting a mass of material items.

Think about it.

Call to Action

Identify a cause or service organization that has meaning to you. Then call them to see how you can volunteer for a day. You might want to recruit a friend or family member to join you. The key is to take action now and to volunteer within the next month. Your soul will rock from the experience!

" "

• • •

I've found that the most difficult experiences of my life have given me the most beauty in the end.

–Olivia Newton-John, Australian-Raised Singer and Actress

Lesson 46
Difficulty Breeds Beauty

My girlfriends and I like to laugh about the fact that life isn't quite like it was depicted in those fairy tales we read as little kids. All the stories ended with that intoxicating phrase "and they lived happily ever after." That simple one-liner planted a belief in my young mind life would always work out somehow, as it did for every fairy tale princess tormented by a wicked witch or hairy ogre.

Once I hit the age of thirty and had weathered some major personal and professional bumps, I started thinking, "What the heck is going on here? Life is not working out the way I planned, and it's pretty difficult at times." Thankfully, I have always been able to muster up the belief that things will work out and I will be happy.

These days, I still hold on to a "happily ever after" ideal, but it's one which is open to the difficulties of daily life and work. I've had my share of hard knocks and rough patches, but I see all dark times as an opportunity to give birth to new beauty in one's life. The most contented people have learned to embrace both the difficult and the "happily ever after" seasons of their journeys because both elements are a natural part of the cycle of life.

How about you? Every difficulty you face can unfold into something beautiful if you persist, muster up a positive vision, and hold on to faith.

Think about it.

Call to Action

If you are having trouble in your life, take out a piece of paper, set your alarm clock for thirty minutes, and write about the challenges. Handwrite your thoughts for maximum benefit. Remember, everyone's challenges are different, so don't judge yourself if you think your difficulties aren't worthy of attention. Write about how you feel and why the experiences are particularly difficult. Then list three to five positives that could come out of the difficultly if you stay the course and focus yourself in the right direction with the right plan and the right people around you.

" "

. . .

*Do you want to be
safe and good, or do you
want to take a chance
and be great?*

–Jimmy Johnson, Former Dallas Cowboys Coach

Lesson 47
Take a Chance

In many aspects of my life, I'm a risk taker. One of the biggest risks I've ever taken was leaving the security of a great job and salary in 2001 to start my own business. I could write pages and pages on the personal and professional rewards I've reaped from putting myself out there and refusing to play it safe.

How about you? Are you willing to step out of your comfort zone and take some chances that could lead you to a more rewarding life? Perhaps you'll take a chance on a new career, a new relationship, a new hobby, or developing a new skill. Don't let fear hold you back. The interesting thing about risk taking is that it builds confidence, and confident people attract great opportunities and successes into their lives.

Risks come in all shapes and sizes. My friend Sue was a teacher and she once told me about a big risk she took in the school lunchroom: she decided to eat with the administrators for once rather than her fellow teachers. Guess what? Sue realized that hanging with the administrators wasn't terror-filled at all, and it helped her to see teaching from a different perspective. Sue is now the principal at another school and loves her job every day. Oh, the difference that risk taking can make.

Think about it.

Call to Action

Stretch out of your comfort zone this week and write down one risk you are willing to take. Start with something small (e.g., standing in a different spot in exercise class). Next, make an action plan, then yell "Geronimo!" and move forward. Happy risk taking.

Part Five

Triumph

" ... "

There is nothing that can
limit me except myself.

–Michael Beckwith, Spiritual Teacher

Lesson 48
It's You Who Limits You

Isn't it interesting how we fault others for our challenges and limitations in life? *You know what I'm talking about.* You hear people say, "I'm overweight because my spouse makes me eat pizza every night for dinner" or "My earning potential has been crushed by the economy" or "I'm unhealthy because of global warming." You get my point.

The wonderful truth is *you* are the only one who limits *you*. I'm not saying better results and success come easy and we're not highly influenced by external factors. Better results in life require hard work and persistence, persistence, persistence. What I *am* saying is people who possess an "anything is possible" attitude and the willingness to take action excel far more in life than those who blame others for their limitations. Don't give away your power.

Think about it.

Call to Action

Whip out a piece of paper and write down *one* area of your life where you are limiting yourself. Perhaps it's how much money you earn or the type of professional position you have or the kind of house you live in or your personal relationships. Then write out your dream result. For example, if you have limited yourself to making $60,000, write that down: *I can only make $60,000.* Then write down your dream result, something like: *I earn $100,000.*

All realities you manifest in your current world begin as a thought. Hold on to the dream result you wrote down and post it in a prominent place where you can read it every day for thirty days. Allowing yourself to think big can be powerful.

" "

• • •

I've missed more than 9,000 shots in my career. I've lost almost 300 games. Twenty-six times, I've been trusted to take the game-winning shot and missed. I've failed over and over and over again in my life. And that is why I succeed.

–Michael Jordan, Former Professional Basketball Player

Lesson 49
Failure Isn't a Bad Thing

Can you imagine being Michael Jordan, on the court in front of millions of fans and television viewers, missing shots and losing games? Most of us would take off running at the first sign of a boo or a hiss.

What made Jordan a true champion was his passion for the game, his persistence, the thousands of hours of practice each year, and his ability to shake off what most people might perceive as failure.

Believe it or not, failure is one ingredient in life that unleashes inner genius, talent, and potential. Most people, however, don't push themselves to excel because of their fear of flopping. Working hard, stepping out of our comfort zones, failing, getting back up, and persisting—these are the traits of a true champion.

You can be among the champions of the world if you so choose. Getting knocked down and failing from time to time are normal parts of life. Once we accept this reality, learning how to pick ourselves up again and getting back out there are the keys to success.

Think about it.

Call to Action

This week, think about an area of your life in which *you know* you can do better. Maybe it has to do with your work or your personal life. Write it down and then define one step that will move you toward success. You can do it.

" "

• • •

Spectacular achievement is always preceded by unspectacular preparation.

–Robert H. Schuller, American Televangelist, Pastor, and Author

Lesson 50
Spectacular You

Have you ever attended a fabulous performance of a musical and been in awe of the actors and their singing voices? Such an experience is the result of years of preparation and hundreds, sometimes thousands, of hours of rehearsal. But when the curtain opens, the audience sees and hears what seems like an effortless performance.

Whether you aim to become a spectacular public speaker, a scratch golfer, an amazing graphic designer, a talented writer—you name it—constant practice, preparation, and sharpening of your skills are the keys to success. There's simply no way around it. If you want something badly enough, you must be willing to develop productive habits and practice them like mad to move toward achieving your goal. This is the road to success, for sure.

Think about it.

Call to Action

Define a goal you would like to accomplish and write it down. If you have indeed made a firm decision to master a skill or knowledge set, assemble your team of mentors and trainers, lay out your practice plan, and get going. Remember, it may take months or years to reach your aspiration. The key is to set your goal, then take action, and enjoy every step of your preparation journey. Trust me, wonderful surprises will meet you along the way.

66 ... 99

People with excellence and integrity are people who finish what they start.

–Joyce Meyer, Author and Speaker

Lesson 51
Finish What You Start

The ability to bring things through to the finish is both a skill and a habit. One of the differentiating factors between winners and everyone else in life is that winners finish what they start.

The message is simple yet powerful: *do what you say you are going to do*. If you started cleaning out clutter in your home or office, have the discipline to finish the project. If you jumped into a new diet or exercise program, don't give up just because changes aren't happening as fast as you would like. If you started looking for a new job but can't find the right fit, keep looking until the best position comes along.

When we do not finish what we've started, we burden ourselves. I know people who have twenty or more unfinished projects, and now they are stuck. There is, however, some great news. When you commit to finishing what you've started, extraordinary things happen in your world. I've seen the magic occur over and over again.

Think about it.

Call to Action

Give yourself a gift this week. Write down a list of projects or intentions that you've started but never finished. Rank them in order of complexity, starting with the easiest. For example, "finish cleaning out my dresser drawers" is the simplest item on my list and "create world peace"—well, I'm going to save that one to finish later. You get my point. Once you've completed your list and ranked each item, tackle the easiest things first, cross them off once done, and go on to the next. You will gain an amazing sense of accomplishment by completing what you started.

66 99

• • •

Ask and it will be given.
Seek and you will find.
Knock and it will be
opened for you.

–Jesus (Luke 11:9, Matthew 7:7)

Lesson 52
Ask, Seek, Knock

We all have the ability to take these three actions: ask, seek, knock. But how many times do we sit around in a funk and feel sorry for ourselves because of what's going on—or not going on—in our personal or professional lives?

A rewarding life requires taking action each and every day. If we want something, we must ask for it, and be specific. If we feel lost, we have to seek and find the way—even when it seems as if we'll never get out of the confusing darkness. And if we want to discover what's on the other side of an unknown, we need to knock and have faith that someone will open the door.

Doesn't it feel great to know that we have so much power to live the lives of our dreams? We have been issued a promise that if we ask, seek, and knock, then we will find and receive. Know what you want, specifically ask for it, practice persistence, and have faith.

So that relationship you want? It's possible. That lifestyle you desire? It's possible. That dream you have? It's possible. The most amazing person to ever walk the face of our earth has given each of us this guarantee.

Think about it.

Call to Action

This week, reflect on something you really want. First, clearly ask for what you want—put it out there as plain as day. Then determine if there's someone in your world who you need to involve in helping you achieve what you desire.

If you need something from someone in order to achieve success, you've got to ask him or her for it, right? Jot down with whom you need to have a productive conversation and define your request. Take action and open up to receive the amazing things awaiting you.

About the Author

Kathleen DuBois is an entrepreneur, writer, strategist, and teacher. She is president of Progressity, Inc., a full-service marketing and creative design firm. In addition, Kathleen serves as an adjunct faculty member in the Department of Communication Studies at West Virginia University.

Kathleen has three passions that drive her every day:

- Being a visionary, adventurer, and dreamer.

- Expressing herself through creativity.

- Inspiring others to become better versions of themselves.

She resides in Charleston, West Virginia and Washington, DC, making the most from every single day. For further information, visit the author's website at www.KathleenDuBois.com.

Start your week off right.

If you like what's in this book, sign up for a free weekly Monday Motivation with Kathleen DuBois. Visit www.KathleenDuBois.com and click on the Monday Motivation icon on the homepage.

Sign up for your FREE Monday Motivation *with* Kathleen J. DuBois

Start your week off right with an inspirational email and call to action!

Epilogue

My hope is that this book helps you bring more love,
joy, and abundance into your life.

I wrote it just for you.

www.ingramcontent.com/pod-product-compliance
Lightning Source LLC
LaVergne TN
LVHW021505080426
835509LV00018B/2415